Make Big Money as a Charcoal Sketch Artist

Secret Method to Make Sketches Quickly With No Talent

By

Kevin Stone

ISBN-13: 978-1500997250

ISBN-10: 1500997250

CONTENTS

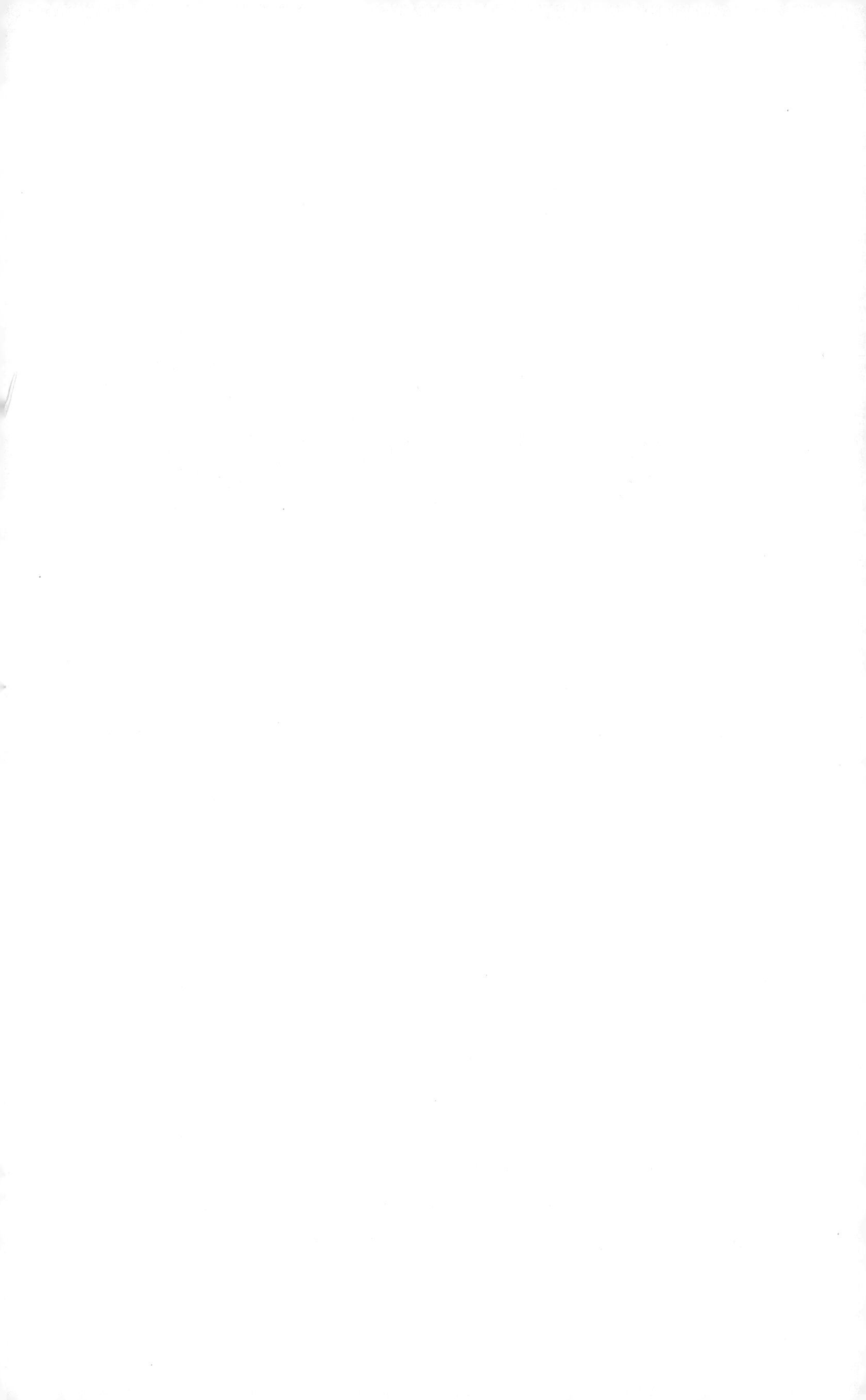

Chapter 1 - Introduction

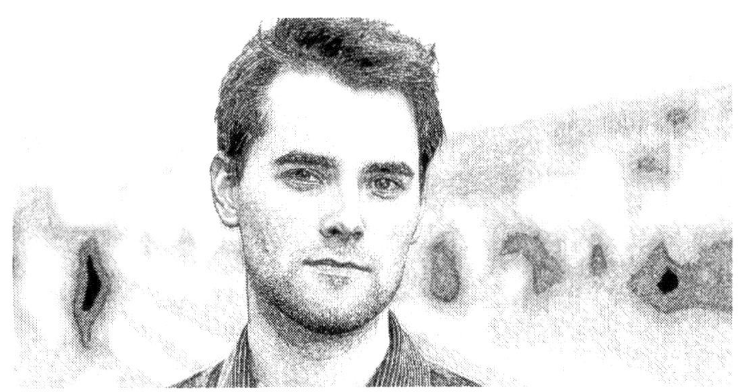

The little known secret of drawing perfect charcoal sketches, without having any art talent, will amaze you! This system will teach you how to draw an exact sketch of a picture on your first attempt. You'll be shocked and amazed at how easy this business is to set up. Your friends, family and customers will adore your new-found talent. Just don't tell them our little secret, ok? As fast as you start showing people your charcoal sketches, the orders will start pouring in. Everyone will want their own sketches. And, since you can draw about four sketches per hour, just imagine how much money you'll make each day. Since charcoal sketches sell for $100 to $500 each, you can make $400 to $2,000 in one hour by drawing four sketches.

This is an easy part-time job, but you can quickly make this business a full-time career. The choice is yours as to whether you want to make a few hundred dollars a week or thousands. I guarantee that you will be able to make exact charcoal sketches of pictures, even on your first try. There is no learning curve with this secret formula and no art talent is required.

Why People Love Sketches

Hand-drawn charcoal sketches are nostalgic and one-of-a-kind. People who see a good sketch usually drop their jaw and mutter oo's and ah's. The simplicity of a detailed, life-like sketch is truly breath-taking. Charcoal sketches are timeless and treasured.

The reason people love hand-drawn sketches is because everyone craves personalized products. People love to buy and cherish personalized items, everything from name bracelets and necklaces to portraits of themselves and their family. There's no question that personalized products are always big selling items, even during rough economies. Everyone wants mementos that capture moments in their life.

You'll discover in your charcoal sketch business that most people will want you to sketch portraits, especially after seeing how life-like your portraits are. However, your customers will also purchase a lot of sketches of their pets, houses, cars and other items that they adore.

Your New Business

You are about to embark on a craft that is simple to make and easy to market. This book will teach you how to make perfect, exact sketches from photographs in just minutes. After you gather a few supplies, you'll be up and running. It is truly the easiest art form to learn, thanks to my secret method. In your first hour, you'll be able to make your first four perfect sketches, since each sketch takes about 15 minutes depending on the complexity of the picture. Everyone will be amazed at how you can make these sketches look so real and life-like.

However, there are other aspects of your business that you'll need to attend to as well. This book will guide you through not only learning how to draw exact sketches (that's the easy part), but will also provide suggestions for marketing your artwork, supply choices, how much to charge for your artwork and other business-related information.

Let's get started!

Chapter 2 - How to Make an Exact Sketch of a Picture

The Big Sketch Art Secret

This is the moment you've been waiting for! Let's discuss how anyone can do realistic, perfect sketches without any artistic talent. As you might know, there are free online websites where you can upload a picture and turn it into a sketch, cartoon, painting, etc. However, while these sites produce nice pictures and sketches, they are NOT hand-drawn with charcoal and would not sell very well on their own since anyone can upload a photo and produce their own sketch for free. However, people WILL pay for a charcoal pencil sketch, signed by an artist. So, use the following steps to create your own charcoal sketches:

1. Create your template. Upload a photo to the website listed below. Although there are several, similar websites to upload pictures and turn them into computer-generated sketches, this site creates the best template for our purposes.

http://www.picturetopeople.org/photo_sketch/realistic_pencil_sketch_photo_effect.html

Once you get to this page, you'll notice that they offer several options for creating an online sketch. However, scroll down to the bottom of the page and you'll notice an area where you can browse for the original picture on your computer and upload it. As long as you are on this page and use the input form at the bottom of this page, it will create the best, realistic and exact computer-generated sketch.

You'll want to keep most of the settings at their default value. However, you should create two sketches, one with the 'smart strokes' option set to 'Extra', and another sketch with the 'smart strokes' option set to 'Normal'. By making two sketches, you will determine which one is best for you to work from. The difference between these options is that heavier lines are drawn when the option is set to 'Extra'. The different affects produced from these two settings has to do with the quality and size of the original picture, as well as the amount of detail in the images. In general, you'll find that sometimes the 'Extra' option produces the best choice, especially for faint or light colored photographs, while the 'Normal' option creates the best sketch for darker photographs.

Next, click on the 'browse' button to locate the original photo on your computer. Once your file is uploaded, click on the 'calculate effect' button. After the sketch is generated by the website and displayed on your screen, you'll need to place your cursor on the sketch, right click and choose the option to save a copy of the sketch to your computer. Next, go back to the previous page, change the 'smart strokes' option from 'Extra' to 'Normal' (or vice versa), and follow the same steps to produce the second computer-generated sketch.

Once you have created the two computer-generated sketches, choose the best sketch to work from. Sometimes you will choose to work from one computer-generated sketch, but for some parts of the picture, you might reference the second photo. So, don't discard the second sketch image just yet.

Original Picture	Computer-generated Sketch
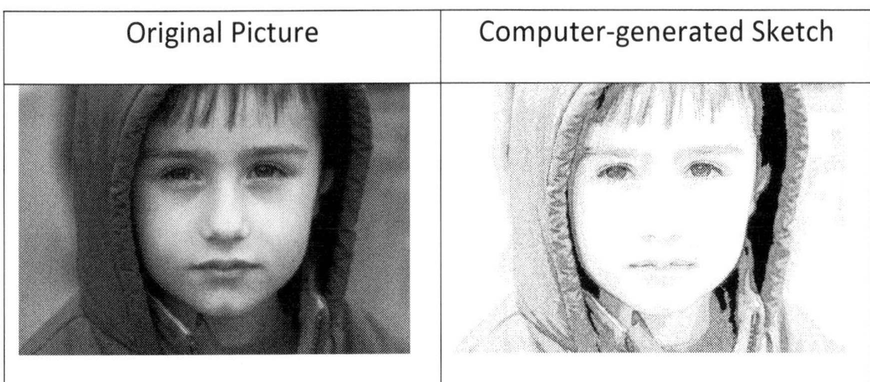	

The maximum size of a picture to upload is 1MG. If the photo you are trying to upload is more than 1MG, then you'll need to resize your photo or change the type of file to a png file in order to reduce the size of the file to less than 1MG. There are numerous free, online websites that allow you to alter pictures in this manner. The best computer-generated sketches come from pictures that are more than 500 X 500 pixels, with 1000 X 1000 being the optimum size.

2. Print a copy of the computer-generated sketch you wish to work with.

3. Place the sketching paper you wish to use for your drawing on a vertical, flat surface such as a wall. An easel might also work as long as the angel of the easel doesn't distort the picture as the image is projected onto the paper.

4. Using a table or other flat surface, place the special tracer projector (detailed in the next section of this chapter) on top of the printed sketch and adjust it so that the image of the sketch displays properly on the paper you mounted on the wall. You might have to move the table and projector closer or further away from the wall until the image projected is centered on the paper.

5. Trace the image with charcoal pencils. Trace the thickest lines of the sketch first, with a blunt charcoal pencil. In a portrait, this usually is the outline of the head and major facial features. Next, use a highly sharpened charcoal pencil to trace the finer detail lines, especially on the face or other focal points of the sketch.

This is the point when you add YOUR STYLE to the sketch. You don't need any special artistic talent to add your own style. Your style is defined by which lines you choose to trace and which lines you don't trace. For example, let's say that the portrait you are tracing is wearing a hat and the hat has many detailed lines in the hat. You might decide to draw the outline of the hat and a few of the detail lines and then to smudge the area inside of the hat instead of drawing each line. I suggest spending some time on the internet viewing charcoal sketches drawn by other artists so that you can learn when other artists 'smudge' and when they draw very detailed lines. The point is that you always want to do something a little different than the original image.

6. Don't forget to sign your sketch when you're finished.

NOTE: Other helpful tips regarding sketches of portraits, landscapes and animals are detailed later in this chapter.

Supplies

There are many options when choosing your supplies. Fortunately, there are cheap options for this business and you don't need very many supplies. You might be able to find all of the necessary supplies at a local arts and crafts store. However, I've outlined the recommended supplies below with clickable links to Amazon. As a business person who is always cautious about overhead, I've found that Amazon consistently has all of the supplies I need and they are always cheaper than local arts and crafts stores.

A good tracer projector is one of your keys to success in this business. Two of the most recommended tracer projectors are detailed below. The first projector is $63.99, but if you're on a tight budget, the second project will work as well and it's only $22.99.

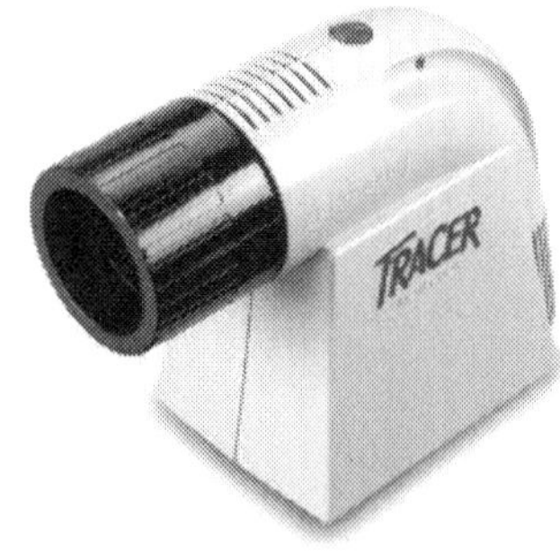

Artograph Tracer Projector and Enlarger - $63.99

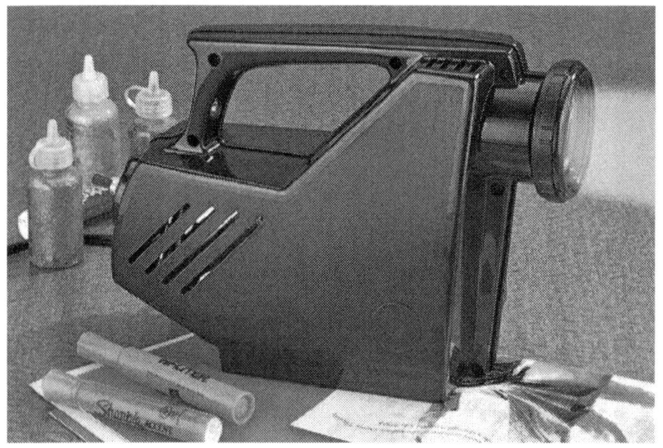

Project - A - Scope Image Projector - $22.99

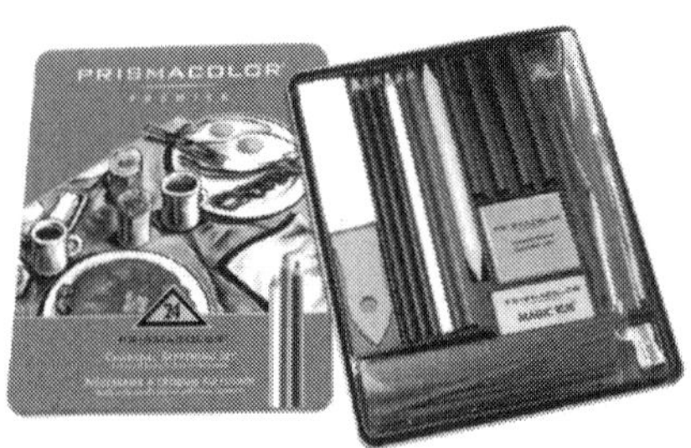

Prismacolor Preimum 24Pc Charcoal Sketch Set - $20.49

If you are just starting out in this business, you can get away with using a smaller set of charcoal pencils. However, you'll later find that moving up to this deluxe set of pencils and accessories will be well worth the money.

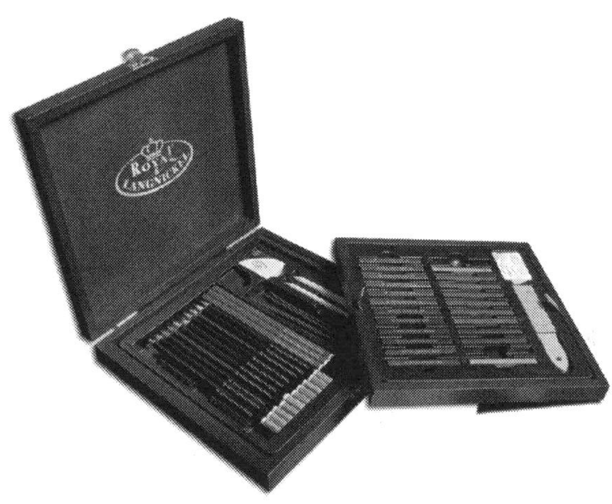

Royal & Langnickel Premier Sketch Pencil Art Set, 51-Piece - $26.95

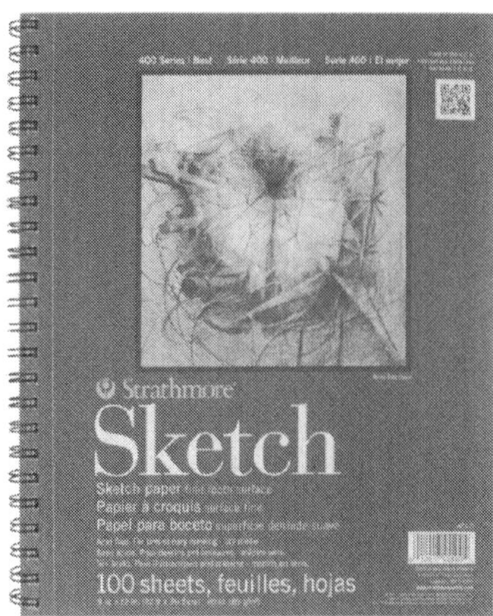

Strathmore Series 400 Sketch Pads 9 in. x 12 in. (pad of 100 sheets) - $9.45

If you choose to use a regular sketch pad for your art, then I highly recommend this sketch pad.

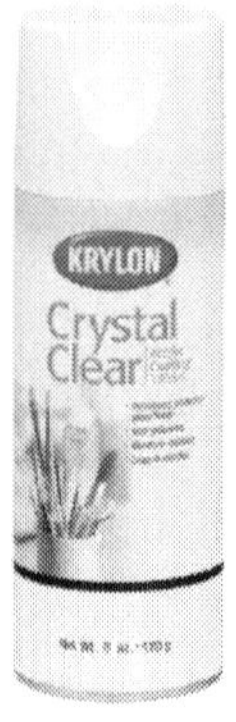

Krylon 6-Ounce Crystal Clear Acrylic Coating Aerosol Spray - $6.99

In the beginning of your career you might get away with not protecting your art work if you're working on a tight budget.

However, I highly recommend you put a protective coating on your charcoal drawings. A smudge or smear on your art work will ruin it. This can of acrylic coating will last a long time, is relatively inexpensive, and will go a long way in protecting your art.

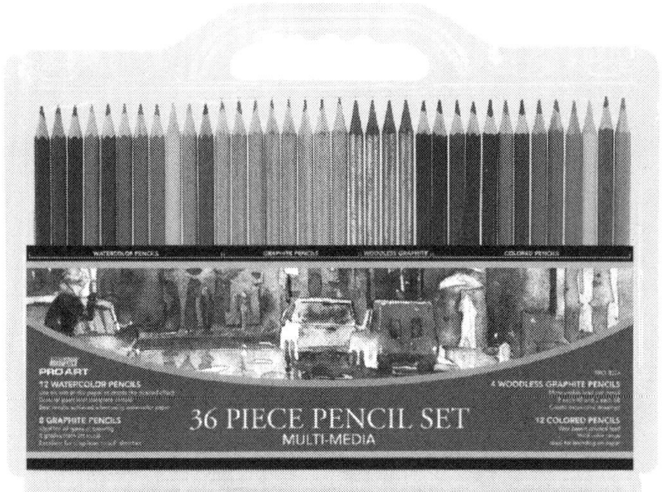

Pro Art 36-Piece Artist Pencil Set - $9.31

Portraits

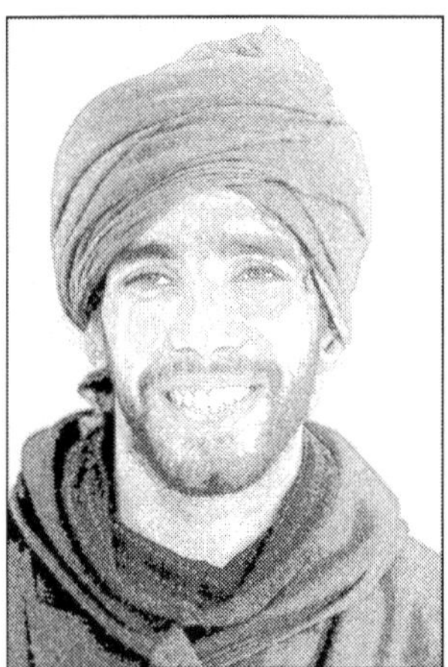

If you're like others in this business, you'll notice that most of your sales will be of portrait sketches. The thought of sketching portraits might sound intimidating at first, but I assure you that they are the easiest picture to sketch. Some tips are provided below:

1. In a portrait, the main facial features are the most important. Be sure to trace the outline of the head, eyes, nose, mouth and ears exactly as it is projected on your paper. Start off with a thicker charcoal pencil or a blunt pencil for the heavier lines. Then, use a highly sharpened pencil to trace the finer details of these features. As long as you exactly trace the main facial features, your sketch will look exactly like the person in the picture. Most of the time you spend on a portrait sketch will be on the facial features.

2. It is not necessary to spend as much time on drawing a detailed sketch of the background or the person's clothes, unless a customer specifically requests otherwise. For example, if the customer requests you to draw a portrait of a man and his new car, then obviously the car must be drawn in great detail. But, you don't necessarily need to spend a lot of time drawing the trees that appear behind the car. Remember, the facial portion of the portrait will look more profound if it is the main focus of the drawing. Some of the most beautiful and striking portrait sketches don't have any background.

3. Ask your customer if they want a sketch of the whole original image or just the portrait of the people in the image.

4. Discourage your customers with providing you original images that are blurry or otherwise low quality pictures. Explain to them that a higher quality image results in a higher quality sketch.

5. The original image of the portrait should be large enough in the image to see facial lines and wrinkles. Otherwise, there may not be enough detail in the image for you to reproduce a sketch that looks exactly like the person. An example of a very poor choice of an image is a snapshot of 200 people in a picture and the customer wants a detailed portrait of only one person in the picture.

Landscapes

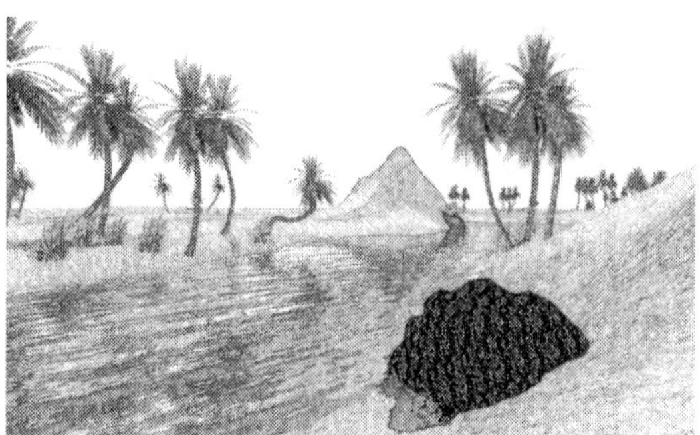

By far, drawing sketches of landscape images are the most time consuming, especially when most of the original picture is of a sky, ocean, or many trees. Luckily, very few clients will ask you to sketch a landscape, unless there is something in the image that is important to them, such as their house. However, I encourage you to find simple pictures of landscapes and draw them as part of your display inventory. Sketches that are already drawn are 'impulsive purchases' and will sell very fast.

As the artist drawing the sketch, it's up to you to look for the main focus in a landscape image and spend most of your time drawing great detail lines of that part of the sketch. For example, the focus might be one large tree on a grassy prairie. In this case, you should draw the tree in great detail, while only faintly sketching the rest of the photo. Remember that you don't need to (nor should you) trace every line of a computer-generated sketch. Save the most detailed drawing for only the focal point(s) of the sketch.

Animals

Sketches of animals, especially pets, are very popular. The suggestions noted above for portraits apply to pets as well. The focus of the sketch is the face, which is where you will spend most of your time drawing the details. Here are some examples of pets and other animal sketches:

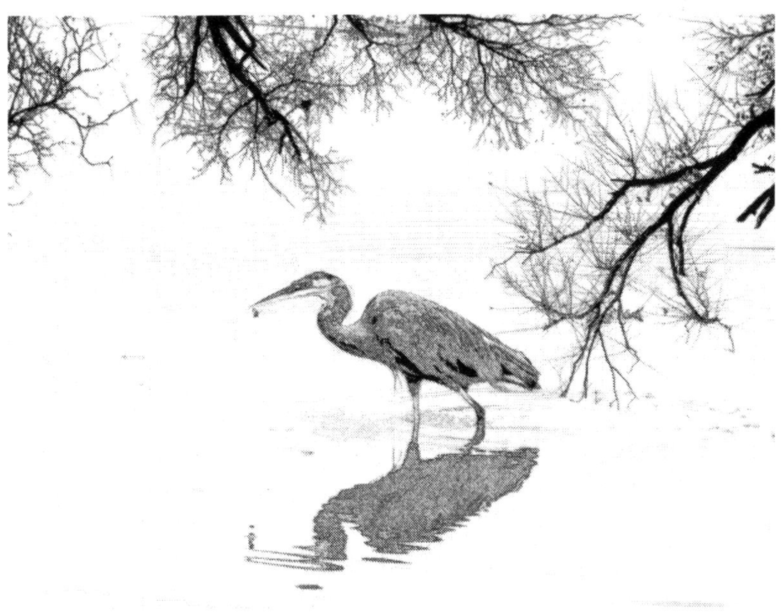

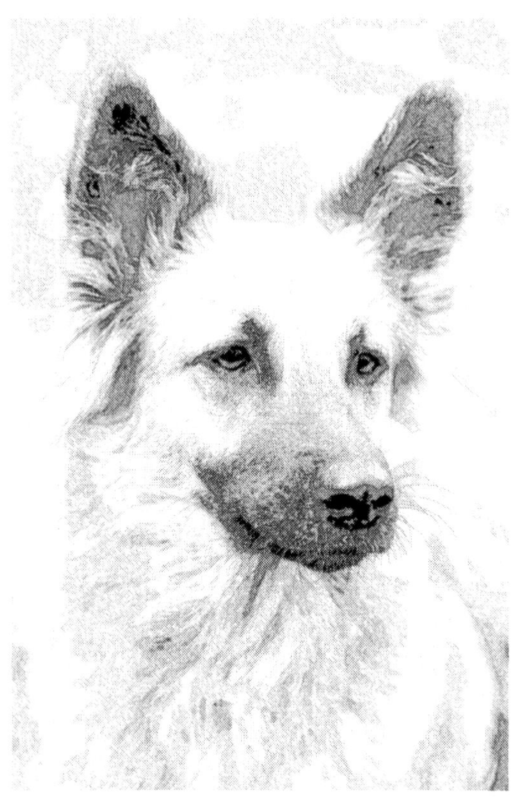

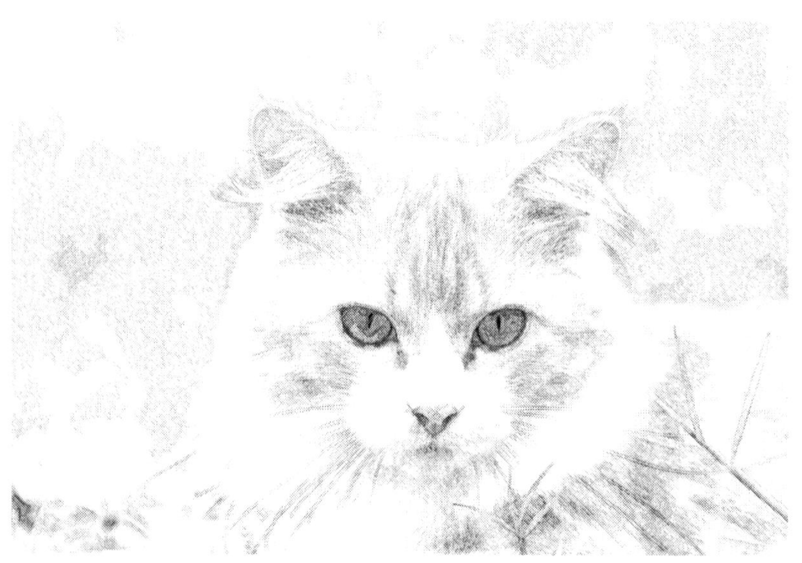

Templates

Sometimes the customer will want the portrait or one's whole body from one image placed in your sketch in a different setting. For example, a customer who has a great photo of their son while he was walking through a junk yard will probably request you sketch him into a different background. For this reason, it's a good idea to have several background templates chosen ahead of time. You should have computer-generated sketches printed ahead of time that you can use at a moment's notice. When you are sketching from two or more images, you should sketch the background first, after you center the projector image on the paper, leaving room for the image from the other photo. So, in the case of a man's body placed in a beach setting, you would first outline the beach background, being careful not to draw in the area you plan on putting the man's body. Next, switch to the projection of the man and draw his body on the paper. Finally, you might wish to switch back to the background projected image to finish drawing the background around the sketch of the man.

You should find images of and make computer-generated sketches for the following backgrounds:

1. Beach

2. Mountains

3. Sky

4. Mount Rushmore. This is a popular sketch requested by

customers. Simply replace one or more of the president's faces with that of your client's sketch.

5. Popular Tourist Sites. People love to see themselves in popular tourist locations. So, gather some templates of places like the Eifel Tower, Niagara Falls, Leaning Tower of Pisa, etc.

Black or Color

Some sketches only use charcoal (black) pencils, while others tend to work with other colors as well. The choice is yours as to whether you want to incorporate colored work, but it's not necessary. I recommend that in the beginning, you stick to just black, as these are the highest sellers by far.

Chapter 3 - How to Start Your Business for Less Than $100

There are many favorable aspects to this business, but the greatest part of starting this business is that you can get a great return on your money, even if you only start your business with less than $100. What other business can you produce something in 15 minutes, with practically no overhead and few supplies, and make $100?

When starting your sketch business, you'll need to first purchase your supplies, especially the projector, charcoal pencils, and something to draw on (such as a pad of heavy stock art paper). We already discussed these in Chapter One. By starting off with the cheaper supplies that we recommended, you can start your business for less than $100.

After you spend the money on your supplies, I recommend you start making sketches for your inventory. We will talk about your inventory in detail later in the book, but for now just realize that you need to sketch a variety of different types of sketches, such as portraits of famous people, landscape scenery, animals, etc. Now, start selling your sketches to family, friends, and other places we recommend later in the book. You'll discover that you will easily be able to recover your initial investment. You'll be tempted to spend the 'easy money' you just made, but in order to ensure long-term success of your business, you should reinvest as much of that initial money as possible in the following areas:

Business Registration

This is essential to running a legitimate business. Depending on your location, it is usually quick and cheap to register your business with your local government. In many locations, you can do this on the internet for less than $50. It is very important to be a registered business, as most flea markets, art shows and other venues are often policed and will require you to show your business registration.

Bookkeeping

Few artists like to spend time maintaining proper financial books for their business. However, it is absolutely essential that you keep good records and receipts. This biggest advice that I can offer is to click on the link below and use the WAVE free accounting software. You can even print invoices directly from your online account. It is not necessary to get an accountant at this point or invest any money in establishing and maintaining your financial bookkeeping.

https://www.waveapps.com/accounting/

It's also highly recommended that you set up a new

checking account. Most tax authorities expect to see your business financial records (income and expenses) in a checking account that does not include personal transactions. You do not need to establish a business checking account, at least at this point in your business, which usually costs more money. It is sufficient to just have a separate account. Also, be sure that all of your expenses and revenue run through this account.

Flea Market Fee

I've listed 'Flea Market Fee' in this chapter because it's a great way to start making money with your sketches. However, many flea markets charge $25 to $35 for a booth, so this should be factored in as part of your initial start-up costs.

Flea markets are a great way to sell your work, but usually you will get less money than if you sold in a more expensive market. But, the idea here is to sell at a local flea market for a day or two, so that you can quickly replenish your business account with more money. You should first draw 30-50 sketches of a variety of types such as portraits of famous people, landscapes and animals. Then, you should discount these sketches so that you can sell them quickly and make money for future expenses. Be sure to put up a sign that advertises your sketches as 50% to 75% off, so that people know they are getting a good deal. For example, a regular sketch that you would normally sell for $100 can be easily sold at a flea market for $25. (This is still good money for a sketch you made in 15 minutes.)

I also recommend that you make smaller sketches as well and price them accordingly. You can quickly make smaller sketches for your inventory and they will sell very well at flea markets, especially if they (even basic) sketches of famous people. Sketches of famous people the size of a post card will sell very quickly at $10 to $15 each.

Remember, that this type of a sale is so that you can raise quick capital for your business. However, you should also start receiving orders for sketches from these customers. I recommend that you charge your regular price for these orders. Only sell your stock inventory sketches at the highly discounted rate. This is an important point! Your customers will turn out to be repeat customers and they will tell their friends and family about your work. If you start off giving high discounts to these 'new' customers, then ALL of your future customers will want the same discount. Stay firm to your policy that only stock inventory sketches are discounted.

Fees Associated with Accepting Credit Cards

Given the high price of sketches, your business will require you to accept credit cards, since most people don't walk around with hundreds of dollars in their pockets. If your business is in the United States, then this is easier to do than you might think. There are many companies that will set you up with a card scanner (usually for free) that you can plug into a smart phone and accept credit cards. The money goes to your checking account and this process has become very easy. Of course you'll need to shop around for the best card reader and service for you, but as of the date of this publication, the 'Square Credit Card Reader' is a very popular and inexpensive choice.

Chapter 4 - How Much to Charge for Your Art

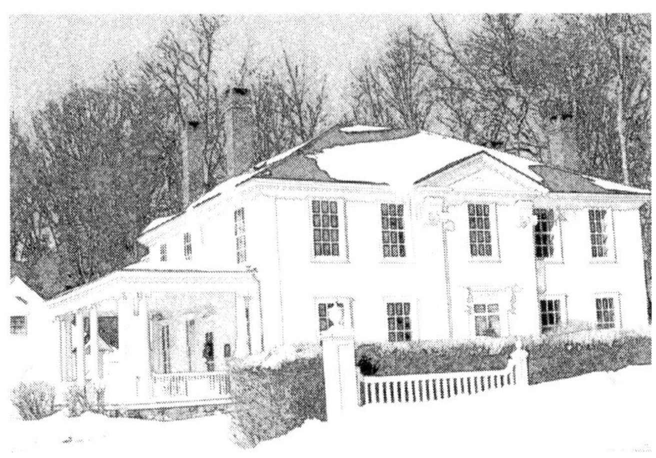

A quick Google search of "charcoal portrait sketch prices" will amaze you with sites that charge a small fortune for charcoal pencil sketches. The average price, as of the date of this publication, is about $150 for a single subject (person or animal) portrait and $300 for a sketch with two subjects. Although, it's common to see sketches that sell for $300 to $500.

There are many factors that affect your pricing structure. A few of them are discussed below.

Size and Number of Subjects

The size of your sketch is the biggest factor in determining how much to charge. The larger the sketch, the higher the price. Here is a sample of how size affects pricing. (NOTE: these prices do not include a frame.)

Size of Paper and Number of Subjects

12x16" single subject - $150

16x20" single subject - $200

20x24" Pet or Family Portraits, single subject - $250

24x36 " single subject - $350

Type of surface

The prices listed in the chart above are for sketches drawn on regular sketch art paper. If you choose to offer sketches on different surfaces, such as a piece of wood, then your prices would change depending on the cost of the surface. As a reference, the regular sketch art paper is about 10 cents per sheet. So obviously, if you choose to use a more expensive surface, then your costs (and selling price) will be greater.

Color

Some sketch artists charge more for color sketches, although the costs of supplies are about the same. Color sketches require more time, thought, experience, and talent. The same website I recommended before (http://picturetopeople.org) has a specific page for creating a computer-generated sketch in color. If you choose to add some color to your sketches, then I recommend using these computer-generated sketches as your template, as they display great color themes to the sketch.

Sales Location and Type of Customer

Where you choose to sell your work and the type of customer affects the price you can reasonably assume to fetch for your art. You'll get less money for your sketches at a flea market than an expensive art show, as an example. Generally, the more money it costs you to sell your art at a particular location, the more you will be able to (and should) sell your artwork.

It's advisable to personally scout potential event and sales locations before you sign up. Your biggest interests in various venues should be the number of people who attend the event and average price of goods sold at the event. The average price of the goods sold by other vendors is the best gauge of how much money you will be able to charge for your artwork. For example, if most of the venders at an event are selling items for less than

$10, then it will be nearly impossible for you to sell a sketch for $300. If this were the case and you really wanted to sell artwork at this type of venue, then you should concentrate on smaller sketches sold at a lower price.

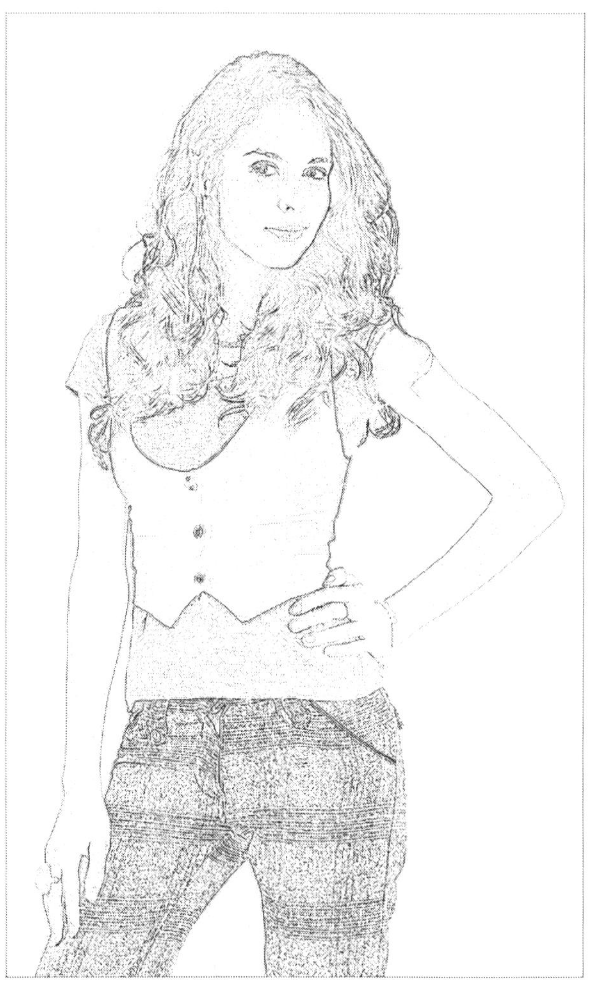

Chapter 5 - Marketing Ideas for Sketches

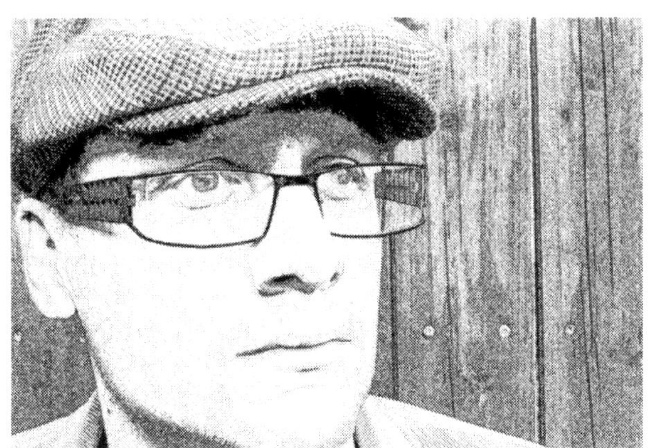

Charcoal sketching is a niche market, as it is a specific medium within the field of art. However, in order to maximize your sales and profits, it's always a good idea to do something that is different than your competition. This chapter provides suggestions on how you can modify your basic sketch art business so that you stand out and are known for something different and special.

Different Surfaces

Most sketch artists only draw on paper. However, you

might want to try several sample sketches (portraits, landscapes, houses) on several surfaces and different sizes and see if there is a market for your sketches on that surface. For example, drawing a sketch of an old barn on wood from an actual old barn is unique and different. Anyone wanting a sketch to remind them of an old barn, perhaps because they played in an old barn as a child, would prefer your sketch of a barn more than someone else's sketch because your sketch is on a real piece of barn wood.

Another different surface that you might want to try is to only sketch on recycled paper. You can take it one step further by easily making your own recycled paper! There are several free websites on the internet that can teach you how to make your own recycled paper.

Be creative and come up with a unique, special surface to draw on. The more creative the idea, the more sketches you will sell at a premium price.

Everything Should Be Made Into a Sketch

Since you are in the business of drawing sketches, everything you do related to advertising should be in the form of sketches. Your business cards and all signs in your sales booth should communicate with the buyer in sketches. If you use paper bags to package small sketches, they should be rubber stamped with a sketch of your business name and a small sketch of your logo. To make these sketches, follow the same instructions for your regular sketches every time you need sketches. For example, after you design an appropriate business card, run it through http://peopletopicture.org to make a sketch image that you can give to your business card printing service.

Draw Your Portraits Inside of Famous Locations

It's a great idea to draw your portraits inside or at a famous location. You should make several of these for your stock inventory, because they are very impulsive. If customers think something is unique and special, they will be more prone to buying the sketch or placing an order for their own. Placing one or more portraits in a Mount Rushmore sketch is one such idea. Or, create a sketch of a loving couple at the Eifel Tower in Paris. You might also try sketching your subject's portrait into a scene with one of their favorite actors or singers. Use your imagination to come up with your own special ideas and you'll reap the rewards of this technique.

Draw Sketches for Christmas Cards

Most people take pride in the Christmas cards they send out each year to family and friends. Offer unique sketches that look great for Christmas cards and you'll have a big seller! You might add a nice quote to the sketch and print them yourself using free software that is widely available on the internet.

It's also a good idea to market specialized Christmas cards that include a sketch of the family.

Be sure to start advertising this service early so that people have time to place their orders. It's advisable to begin selling these personalized Christmas cards as early as August.

Sketches of Famous People

Why do sketches of famous people? Because, they sell! People are famous because people like them and people buy what they like. So, it just makes sense to offer your customers sketches of famous people.

I recommend that artists starting off in this business offer a wide selection of sketches to improve the likelihood of quick sales. However, there are times when artists wish to specialize in a particular type of sketch from the beginning of their career for a variety of reasons. For instance, for the artist who doesn't want to deal with taking orders and delivering the final sketch, it is a good idea to specialize in an area where all of the sketches are drawn in advance. If this situation applies to you, then I recommend starting off specializing in sketches of famous people. Pictures of famous people are abundant and you can easily acquire these pictures online.

Even if you choose NOT to specialize in this area, I recommend that your stock inventory consist of sketches of famous people. Here's a list of famous people categories you should consider:

1. Actors and Singers. These are generally best sellers. Offer sketches of the most current and popular actors and singers as well as a mix of historic actors and singers, such as Elvis, Marilyn Monroe, John Wayne, etc.

2. Presidents and famous politicians. A sketch of Abe Lincoln or George Washington is as popular as a sketch of the current president. You should stock sketches of at least the current and three past presidents.

3. Famous Athletes. Just about everyone has a famous athlete and would buy a sketch of that person. Offer sketches of the most popular athletes in your area, such as stars of the closest professional football and basketball team.

4. Famous Religious figures. Sketches of famous religious figures are also hot sellers. Consider stocking sketches of these famous figures, such as the current Pope, Jesus, Moses, Mother Mary, Mother Theresa, and the dahlia Lama.

Chapter 6 - Where to Market Your Sketches

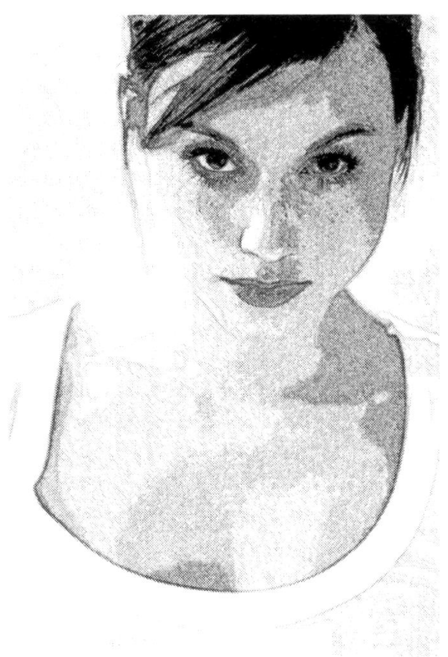

Friends and Family

We'll start off this chapter by discussing friends and family, as they relate to your business. Let's face it, you might talk your mother into buying one of your sketches, but the rest of your family and friends will probably not be interested. So, don't expect them to come running to your door with hundreds of dollars. However, your family and friends can be a great source of free advertising for you, so it's important that you maximize this opportunity.

It might sound like a lot of work, but I encourage you to give a free sketch to each member of your family and all of your friends. You can do this in the beginning of your new career as a sketch artist, or you can gradually give away sketches during special occasions such as birthdays.

They will feel obligated to hang them in their houses and will be inclined to talk about your talents to other people. It's the OTHER people who will pay you good money for your sketches and become regular customers.

Sell Online or Offline?

When considering potential ways to market your sketches, you must first decide if you want to exclusively sell your sketches online, offline, or a combination of both. There are pros and cons to each method and it's usually just a matter of taste and the amount of time you have to invest in marketing. Some people prefer to set up a booth to sell their sketches and don't want to be bothered with a lot of advertising. Other artists prefer to sell their work online to avoid the person-to-person interaction, as an example.

However, if you want to 'reach the masses' and sell as

many of your sketches as possible, then online sales are the best way to do it. The internet can reach billions of potential customers compared to a thousand or so people at a flea market or craft fair. However, the choice is yours.

Offline Sales

To sell your sketches offline, consider the following suggestions:

1. Flea Markets. As I mentioned earlier in the book, flea markets are a great way to quickly sell sketches. Although the price of your sketches will be lower, you'll usually make a lot of money in just one day. I recommend that every new artist begin by selling in a flea market. It's a great way to gauge what customers are interested in within your local area. You might be surprised in the types of sketches your local market buys the most of. The cost of setting up a table or booth at a local flea market is usually very reasonable. It pays to do some online research about how to set up a good booth at a flea market. The more professional your booth looks, the more sales you'll receive. You don't have to spend a lot of money preparing your booth, but there are some good ideas to know about before you embark on this adventure.

2. Schools. High Schools and colleges can really boost your sales. Setting up booths at local school events are a

productive and inexpensive way to get sales. Be sure to offer sketches of the name of the school or one of its sports teams. That is always a big hit with students.

3. Fundraisers are a great way to sell a lot of artwork, because the organization conducting the fundraising event does all of the advertising for you. You will need to give them a digital photo-copy of your brochure and order forms for fundraising events that require members to get the sales and send you the orders. Expect to give the fundraising event between 30% and 50% of the sales price. So, adjust your prices accordingly.

4. Local Establishments. There are many potential local establishments that will re-sell your sketches. Most of these include local museums, art galleries, specialty art stores, etc. this option will require you to seek out these potential markets and then approach the owner or director of the establishment. However, many artists find these types of markets to be very lucrative with a lot of repeat business.

Online Sales

There are many opportunities to sell your sketches online. Some require more work on your part than others, but the internet has a customer base of billions of people and you'll discover it is worth all the effort you put into your online business.

You've probably heard about how sites such as Twitter, Facebook and other similar sites can greatly increase your sales. But, let me first state that you should begin with a main webpage that shows your art, their prices, and has the ability for people to purchase your work. This is the most important part. Other sites, such as a Twitter and Facebook act as funnels to attract people whom you will direct to your main website to make purchases.

There are many free resources on the internet, to include YouTube videos on how to create free websites and how to funnel traffic from social media websites and blogs to your main webpage. These resources seem endless and quite daunting for the beginner, so I suggest you create your main webpage first and then gradually work on your funnel.

Ebay

Some artists prefer to sell their work on websites that are already established. This is an attractive way to sell artwork for many people and doesn't involve a lot of work on the part of the artist. Ebay is one such website. After you set up an Ebay account, you only need to list each piece of artwork and upload a good quality photo and Ebay does most of the work for you. Be sure to set your auction price at the lowest point you are willing to get for your sketch. For example, you might list an sketch of Elvis for $25 that you hope will end up selling for much more. It's important that you not lose money on Ebay, so set the initial price low enough that you will at least recoup enough money for your time and materials.

Etsy

Etsy is a site that is similar to Ebay, but doesn't have an auction capability and Etsy is only for artists. Many artists use their Etsy webpage as their main site where they sell all of their art.

Facebook

Unlike Ebay and Etsy, Facebook is not a place where you can sell your artwork directly. It is more of a funnel to get people to go to your main website and make a purchase. You should consider building a Facebook Fan Page for sketches and make regular posts. Within those posts, you can nudge readers to visit your store and purchase your sketches. This is a powerful funnel for sales and is very popular. I highly encourage you to investigate how to build a Facebook Fan Page by reading free articles and YouTube videos on the internet.

Chapter 7 - Final Thoughts

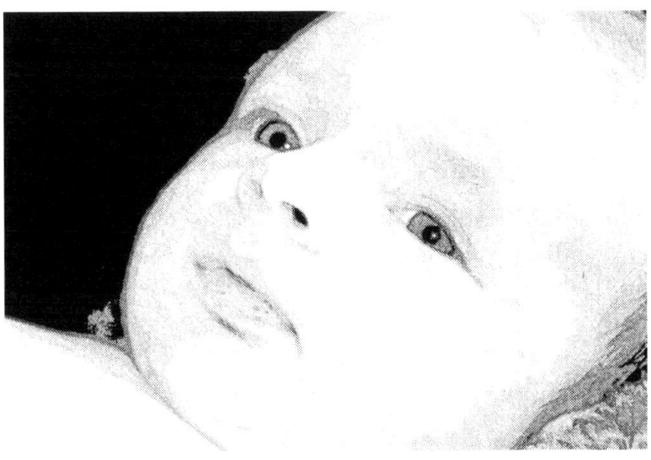

Congratulations on your future success as a professional sketch artist! Just as the many people before you have learned, you will discover that this is a very profitable business. However, as with any business, your success is determined by the level of dedication and work that you put into your business. I encourage you to constantly strive to be better and different than your competition. Best wishes!

I hope this book was inspirational and helpful. Please take the time to return to the amazon.com page where you bought this book and leave a review of this book. Thank you! I really appreciate it.

Printed in Great Britain
by Amazon